The Toddler's handbook

with over 100 Words
that every kid should know

BY DAYNA MARTIN

ENGAGE BOOKS
VANCOUVER

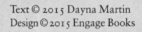

e ENGAGE BOOKS

Mailing address
PO BOX 4608
Main Station Terminal
349 West Georgia Street
Vancouver, BC
Canada, V6B 4A1

www.engagebooks.ca

Written & compiled by: Dayna Martin
Edited & designed by: A.R. Roumanis
Photos supplied by: Shutterstock

FIRST EDITION / FIRST PRINTING

LIBRARY AND ARCHIVES CANADA CATALOGUING IN PUBLICATION

Martin, Dayna, 1983–, author
    The toddler's handbook : numbers, colors, shapes, sizes, ABC animals,
opposites, and sounds, with over 100 words that every kid should know /
written by Dayna Martin ; edited by A.R. Roumanis.

Issued in print and electronic formats.
ISBN 978-1-77226-106-6 (bound). –
ISBN 978-1-77226-105-9 (paperback). –
ISBN 978-1-77226-107-3 (pdf). –
ISBN 978-1-77226-108-0 (epub). –
ISBN 978-1-77226-109-7 (kindle)

1. Vocabulary – Juvenile literature.
2. Word recognition – Juvenile literature.
I. Roumanis, A. R., editor
II. Title.

PE1449.M375 2015   J428.1   C2015-905050-2
                                                            C2015-905051-0

4
ABCs

11
NUMBERS

14
COLORS

16
OPPOSITES

22
SHAPES

24
SOUNDS

28
ACTIONS

30
EMOTIONS

32
SPORTS

34
ENGINES

36
SIZES

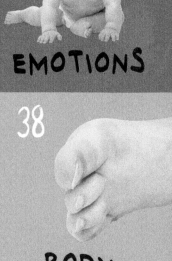
38
BODY

40
TABLEWARE

42
CLOTHES

44
BATH TIME

45
BED TIME

3

Aa

Alligator

Bb

4 Bear

Cc

Cat

Dd

Dog

Ee

Elephant

Ff

Fox

Gg

Goat 5

Hh

Horse

Ii

Iguana

Jj

Jaguar

6

Kk

Koala

Ll

Lion

Mm

Mouse

Nn

Newt 7

Oo

Otter

Pp

Pig

Qq

8 Quail

Rr

Rabbit

S s

Seal

T t

Tiger

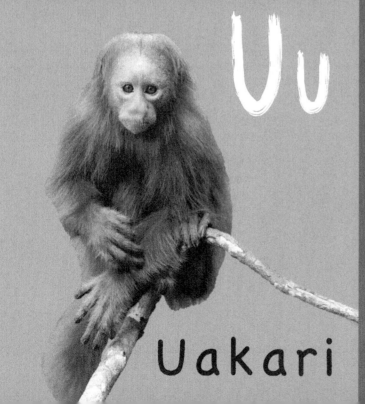

U u

Uakari

V v

Vulture 9

Ww

Weasel

Xx

X-ray fish

Yy

Yak

Zz

Zebra

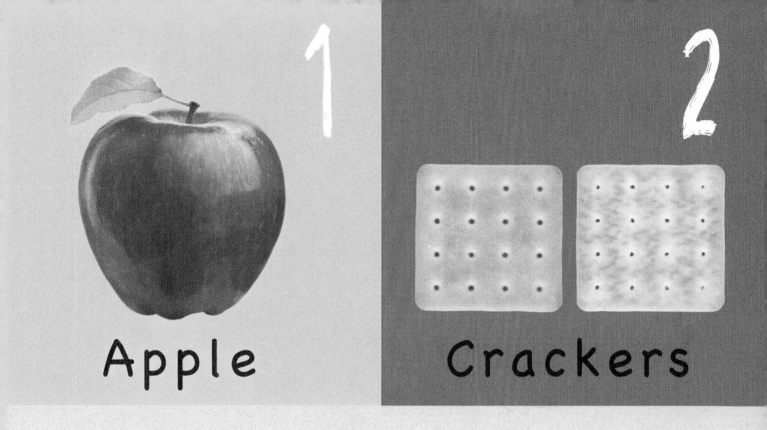

1

Apple

2

Crackers

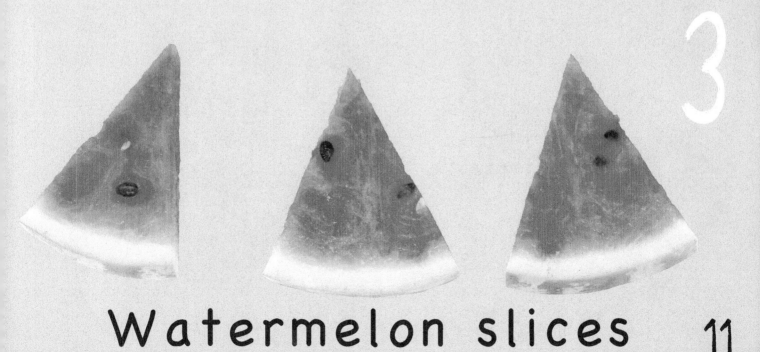

3

Watermelon slices

4

Strawberries

5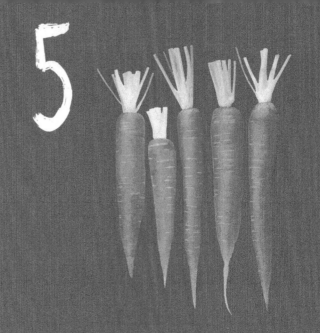

Carrots

6

Tomatoes

7

Pumpkins

8

Fruit slices

9

Potatoes

10

Cookies 13

Rainbow

Red

Fire Hydrant

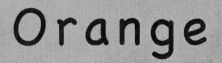

Orange

14 Fish

Yellow

Bananas

Green

Lego

Blue

Balloon

Indigo

Butterfly

Violet

Broom

15

Up

Down

16 In

Out

Hot

Cold

Wet

Dry

Front

Back

18 On

Off

Open

Closed

Empty

Full

19

Safe

Dangerous

20 Big

Small

Asleep

Awake

Long

Short 21

Circle

Tire

Square

Blocks

Rectangle

22 Pan

Triangle

Pizza

Cone

Tree

Star

Starfish

Oval

Easter egg

Heart

Leaf   23

Ah-choo

Sneeze

Quack

Duck

Moo

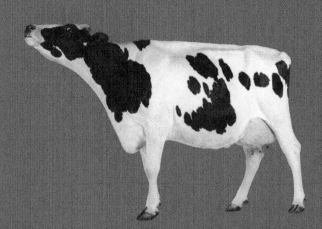

Cow

Ring

Phone

Ooh-ooh-ahh-ahh  Ribbit

Frog

Shh

Monkey Hush 25

cock-a-doodle-doo

Boom

Rooster

Drums

Hiss

26

Snake

Hoot

Owl

Buzz

Bumblebee

Clap

Hands

Baa

Lamb

Crawl

Roll

28 Walk

Run

Hop

Ride

Kiss

Jump 29

Happy

Sad

Angry

Scared

Frustration

Surprise

Shock

Brave

31

Baseball

Basketball

32 Tennis

Soccer

Badminton

Football

Volleyball

Golf 33

Fire truck

34　Car

Race car

Helicopter

Airplane

Cement truck

Truck   35

Flower

Small   Medium   Large

Berry

36 Small   Medium   Large

Leaf

Large Medium Small

Toy

Large Medium Small 37

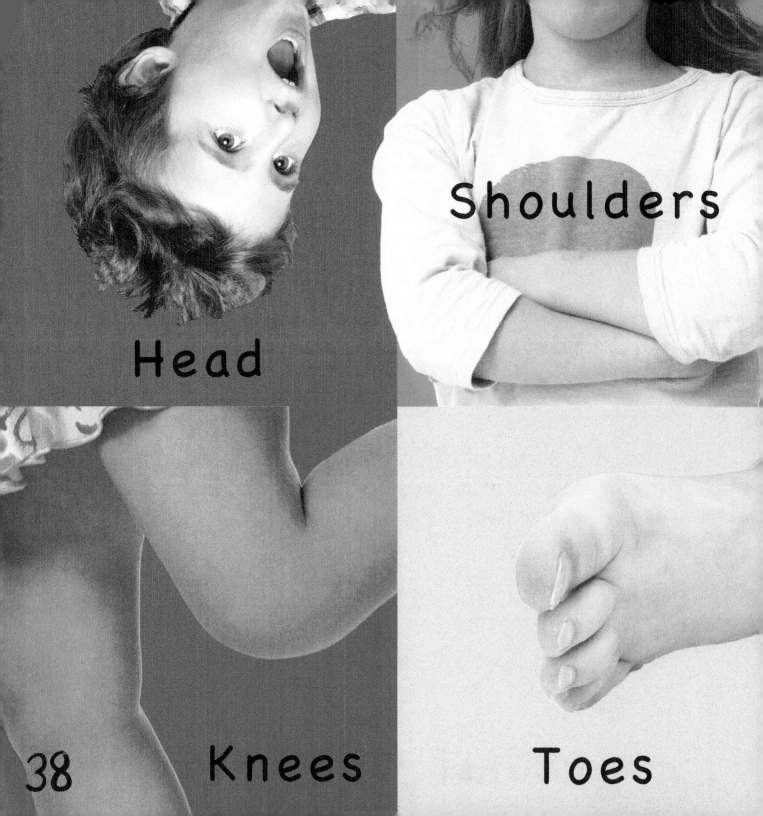

Head

Shoulders

38 Knees

Toes

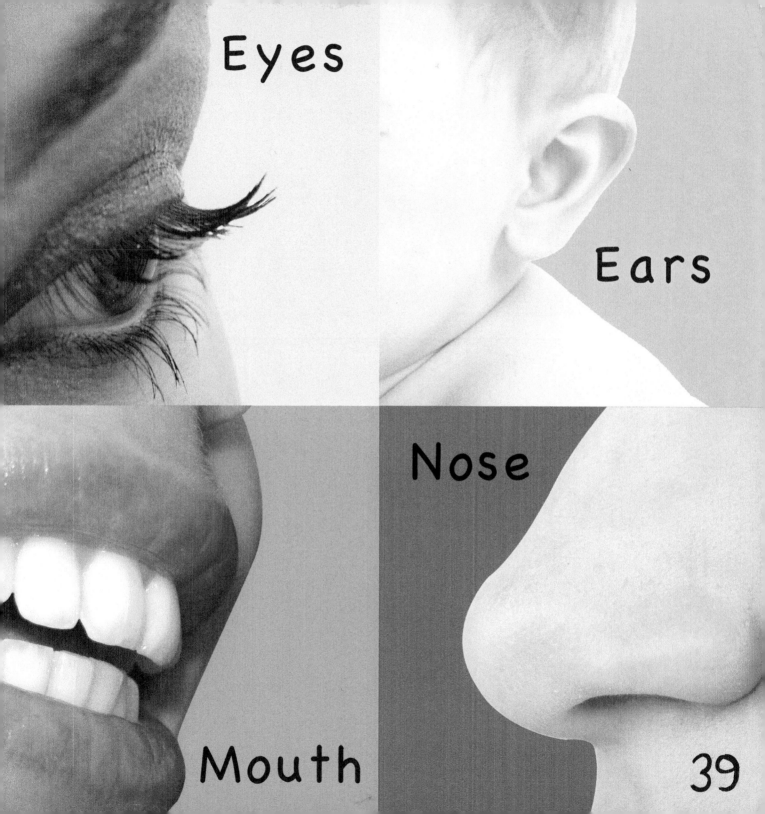

Eyes

Ears

Nose

Mouth

39

Sippy cup

Bowl

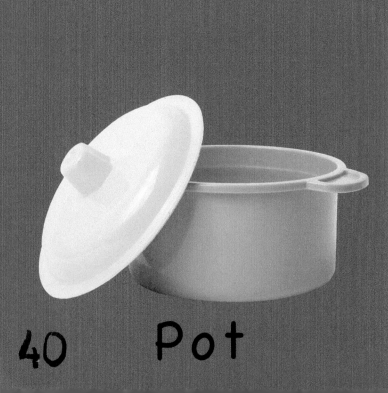

40 Pot

Cup

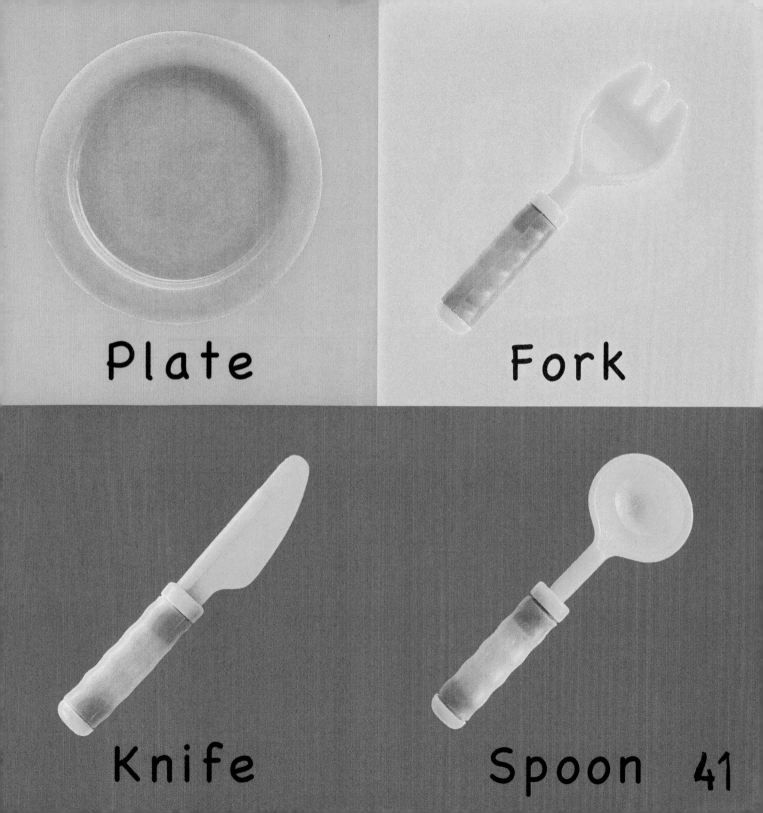

Plate

Fork

Knife

Spoon 41

Hat

Shirt

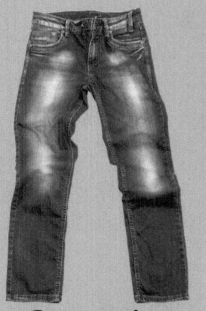

42 Pants

Shorts

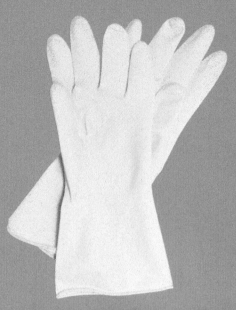

Gloves

Sunglasses

Socks

Shoes

43

Bath time

Bath

Soap

Rubber duck

Brush

Book

Potty

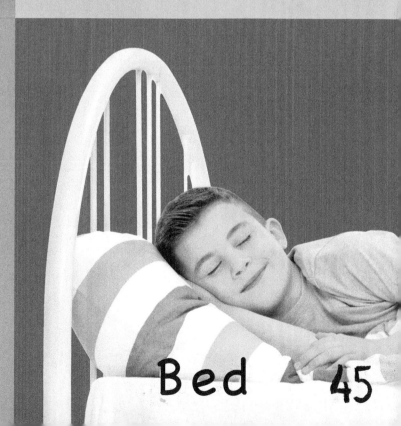

Bed   45

THE TODDLER'S HANDBOOK

activity

Match the following to the pictures below. Can you find **7 pumpkins**, a hooting owl, a rainbow, a baseball, a lion, square blocks, a sad boy, a helicopter, and shoes?

Answer: helicopter

Answer: shoes

Answer: lion

Answer: baseball

Answer: 7 pumpkins

Answer: sad boy

Answer: hooting owl

Answer: square blocks

Answer: rainbow

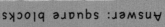

46

CPSIA information can be obtained at www.ICGtesting.com
Printed in the USA
BVOW07s0119030116

431533BV00033BA/288/P